W0113458

better together*

*This book is best read together, grownup and kid.

 akidsco.com

a
kids
book
about

a kids book about

kindness online

by Nehal Dalgliesh

A Kids Co.
Editor Emma Wolf
Designer Rick DeLucco
Creative Director Rick DeLucco
Studio Manager Kenya Feldes
Sales Director Melanie Wilkins
Head of Books Jennifer Goldstein
CEO and Founder Jelani Memory

DK
Delhi Technical Team Bimlesh Tiwary Pushpak Tyagi, Rakesh Kumar
Senior Production Editor Jennifer Murray
Senior Production Controller Louise Minihane
Senior Acquisitions Editor Katy Flint
Acquisitions Project Editor Sara Forster
Managing Art Editor Vicky Short
Managing Director, Licensing Mark Searle

First American edition, 2025
Published in the United States by DK Publishing, 1745 Broadway, 20th Floor,
New York, NY 10019

First published in Great Britain in 2025 by
Dorling Kindersley Limited, 20 Vauxhall Bridge Road, London SW1V 2SA
A Penguin Random House Company

The authorised representative in the EEA is
Dorling Kindersley Verlag GmbH. Arnulfstr. 124, 80636 Munich, Germany

Copyright © 2025 Dorling Kindersley Limited
A Kids Book About, Kids Are Ready, and the colophon 'a' are trademarks of A Kids Book About, Inc.
10 9 8 7 6 5 4 3 2 1
001-349907-April/2025
All rights reserved.
No part of this publication may be reproduced, stored in or introduced into a retrieval system,
or transmitted, in any form, or by any means (electronic, mechanical, photocopying, recording,
or otherwise), without the prior written permission of the copyright owner.

A catalog record for this book is available from the Library of Congress.
A CIP catalogue record for this book is available from the British Library.
ISBN: 978-0-2417-4365-2

DK books are available at special discounts when purchased in bulk for sales
promotions, premiums, fund-raising, or education use. For details, contact:
DK Publishing Special Markets, 1745 Broadway, 20th Floor, New York, NY 10019
SpecialSales@dk.com

Printed and bound in China
www.dk.com
akidsco.com

MIX
Paper | Supporting
responsible forestry
FSC™ C018179

This book was made with Forest
Stewardship Council™ certified
paper – one small step in DK's
commitment to a sustainable future.
**Learn more at www.dk.com/uk/
information/sustainability**

For my wonderful children,
and all kids, who I know can make the
online world a better place.

Intro
for grownups

Tired of seeing an online world full of hate, cyberbullying, and negativity? Yeah, me too!

Hi, I'm Nehal. I wrote this book to introduce kids to the basic concepts of kindness online through empathy, respect, and responsible behavior. Creating a kind world online is about transferring the same etiquette we use in the real world to the digital space, whether it's through gaming, social media, or anything else. It's about understanding that our online identities are part of who we are, and though the online space may feel like a free-for-all with no rules or boundaries, in choosing kindness we help shape a more positive and inclusive online world.

I hope this book will inspire kids to think about the impact of their words and interactions, consider others' feelings, and encourage them to think twice before they hit send.

The digital world is here to stay—let's help make it a kind one!

Imagine...

you're walking to school.

Your friend sees you, smiles, and waves at you.

You wait for the stoplight to show you when to cross the road together, safely.

Now...
what if your friend
didn't smile or wave?

What if they *glared* or
SHOUTED at you instead?

How would that make you feel?

And what if there were no red lights... or any lights at all? Or crosswalks?

What if no one cared about the rules of the road or anyone else around them?

How scary would that be?

You might be wondering why I'm talking about traffic rules in a book about kindness online.

Well, they're actually more connected than you think.

The truth is, we have a lot of rules for how we're meant to act in the "real world."

They keep us safe and help us all get along.

But, people don't always
know how to act online.

And I have something
really important
to tell you:

The way we interact with others in person,

→ **is just as important** ←
as how we interact
with others online.

It matters that we're kind because every time we use our screens, we're shaping the online world.

Do we want to live
in a world that's
chaotic, unfriendly,
and unsafe? One
without stoplights?

R, do we want to live in a world where people are caring, respect one another, and want to help each other grow?

I, personally, would like
to live in the second one!

A world filled with kindness!

So, what does it look like
to be a kind person online?

Kindness is an action that comes from having compassion for who you're communicating with.

It means recognizing that online...

real people are on the other side of the screen.

Being kind online also means understanding that each person has different experiences and boundaries.

Have you ever heard the saying, "Throw kindness around like confetti."?

Sure, it's good to spread kindness around as much as possible, but...

what if someone only likes blue confetti, not a bunch of different colors?

What if they don't like confetti at all?

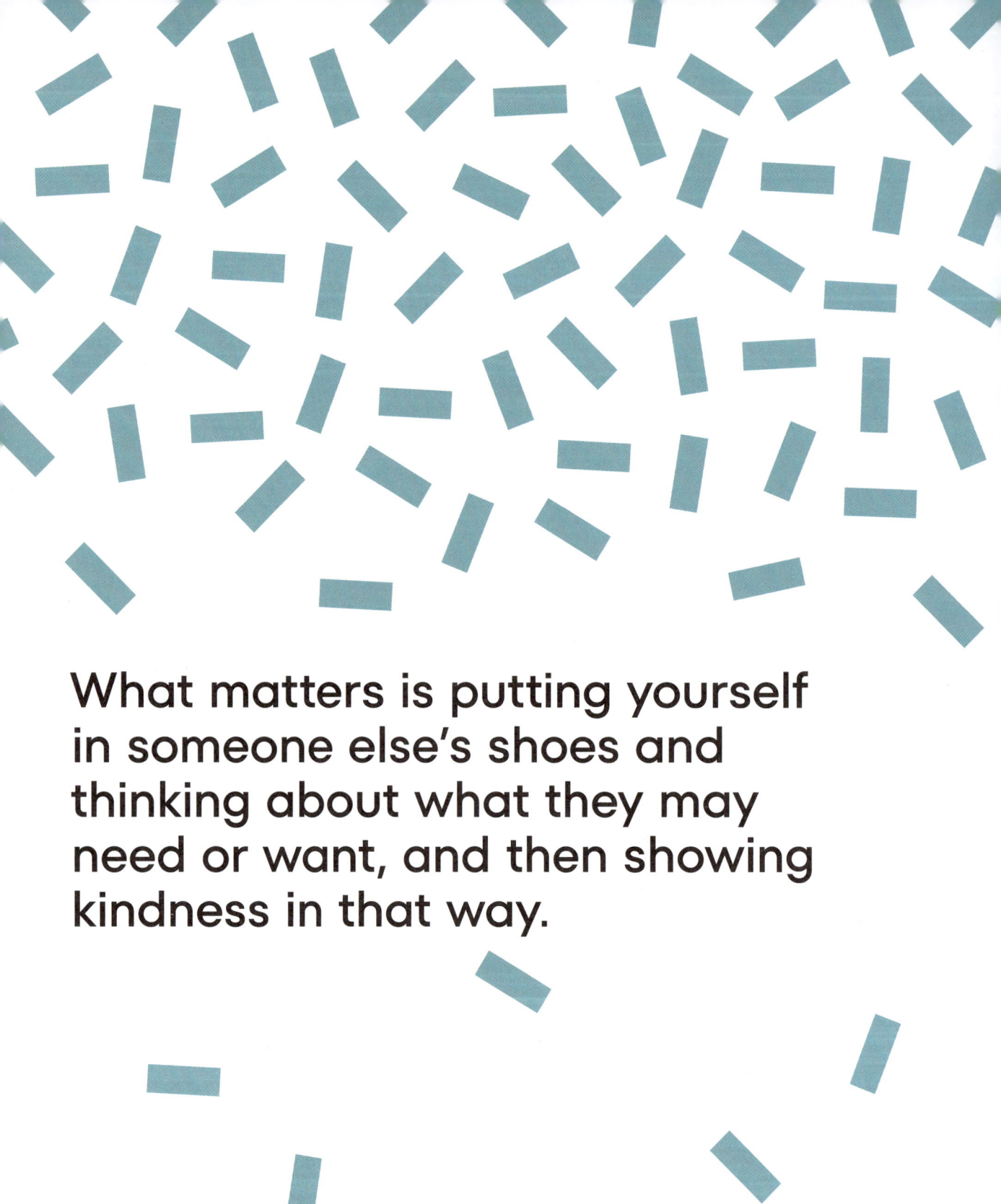

What matters is putting yourself in someone else's shoes and thinking about what they may need or want, and then showing kindness in that way.

Like giving them the blue confetti! Or a hug instead of confetti, if that's what they like best.

Kindness online might mean...

Noticing someone is sad, and leaving them a positive message.

"Hey! You're awesome!"

2.

Remembering the words we use can impact how people feel.

Typing in **ALL-CAPS CAN SEEM LIKE YOU'RE SHOUTING!**

Adding a smiley face emoji can feel friendly. **:)**

Understanding that we're all different and like different things.

It's always kind to keep scrolling instead of leaving not-so-nice messages!

4.

Asking permission to share
a photo or information
about someone online.

**Are they pretty active online?
Or do they like to be
more private?**

5.

Finding out if what you're sharing is real or made up.

Sometimes, sharing made-up things can really hurt people, their families, and their friends.

6.

Posting good stuff that
makes people smile!

=:) :-) =:) :-)

7.

Being kind to yourself, too, by thinking about your own feelings.

Kindness starts within.

I bet you can think of lots of other ways to be kind online!

And what about when you see other people → being unkind online? ← How should you respond?

It's always good to stop
and think before you react.

Talking with a trustworthy grownup is a great place to start.

They can help you decide whether to ignore and move on, block or report, or figure out the best way to use your voice!

We always stop, look, and think before we cross the road, right?

Before you share anything online, it's a good idea to pause and consider:

➡ **Who's reading it?**

➡ **Is it helpful?**

➡ **Does it make people feel included and good about themselves?**

➡ **Am I being the best version of myself when I post online?**

There are lots of things to think about!

But that's because...

→ **how
we are
online**

i

↓

**is super
important.**

When we choose kindness, we're helping create an environment that feels good, safe, and welcoming for everyone.

And it's important to do that in our neighborhoods, our classrooms, and also in our spaces in the digital world.

Did you know that when we see acts of kindness, we're all more likely to copy those acts and spread even

more
kindi

ness

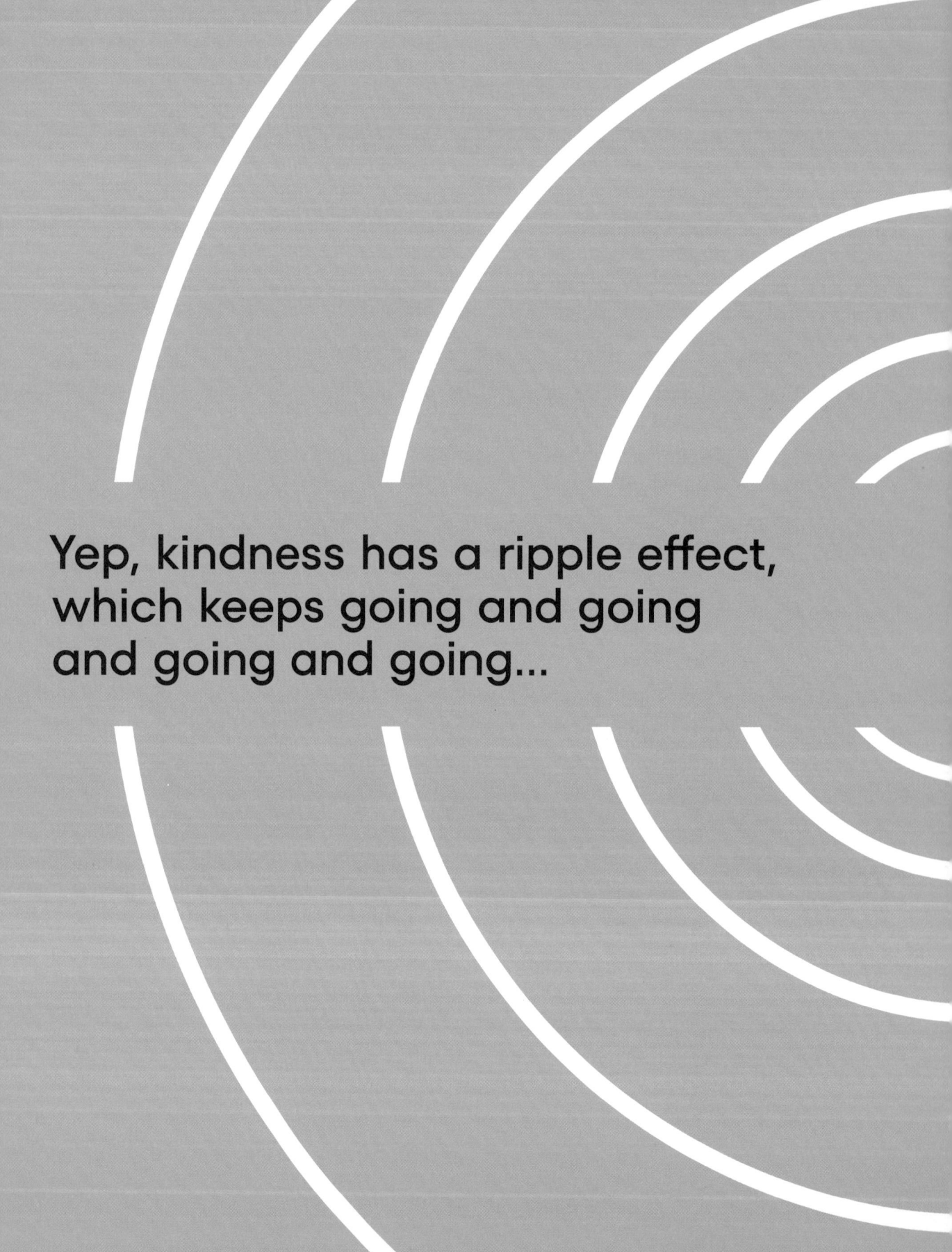

Yep, kindness has a ripple effect,
which keeps going and going
and going and going...

touching more people, and transforming our worlds (online and everywhere) into better places.

So, what sort of online world
do you want to live in?

How

will

you

help

create

it?

It might take some practice.

Consistently putting your
best self forward takes
a lot of thought and care!

But the more you do it,
the easier it becomes.

It's up
to you to
decide how
you'll make
the online
world a
better place
every time
you use a
screen. I

→ You ← have the power.

Use it wisely.
Use it kindly.

Outro
for grownups

Your conversations about kindness online are just getting started, dear grownup! I encourage you to think about how you can apply the concepts from this book to everyday situations with your kids:

- Ask how they feel when someone is kind or unkind to them.

- Explore games and online platforms together, highlighting examples of kindness and unkindness.

- Help them learn how to use more positive language online.

- Remind them that *not* commenting is always an option!

- Help find common ground with others who have different likes or opinions.

- Talk about online safety and personal boundaries.

- Reinforce the idea that every online interaction leaves a digital footprint (yes, even when we delete!).

- Ask if they're proud of the person they are online.

- Remind them that they're human, and while kindness is an ideal we can all strive to achieve, we might not always get it right—and that's OK.

You've got this!

About The Author

Nehal Dalgliesh (she/her) wrote this book to help kids and their grownups think about how to make the online world a better place. As an accomplished journalist and the visionary founder of positive news platform CelebrityKind, she has dedicated her career to fostering a kind online environment.

While it isn't always easy, (because hey, we're all human!), Nehal believes kindness is a choice we can try to make with every interaction, and one that can completely transform the online space.

This book aims to help kids navigate a fast-developing digital world with their hearts, inspiring and empowering the next generation to be kind and compassionate members of the online community.

    @celebritykind @nehaldal

Made to empower.

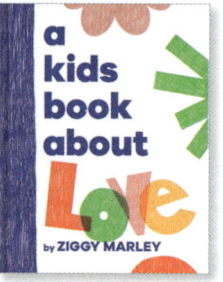

Discover more at akidsco.com